60 Classic Indoor Games

This edition first published in the United Kingdom in 2020 by
Collins and Brown
43 Great Ormond Street
London
WC1N 3HZ

An imprint of Pavilion Books Company Ltd

Distributed in the United States and Canada by
Sterling Publishing Co., Inc. 1166 Avenue of the Americas, New York, NY 10036

ISBN 978-1-91116-355-8

A CIP catalogue record for this book is available from the British Library.

10 9 8 7 6 5 4 3 2 1

Reproduction by Mission Productions Ltd, Hong Kong
Printed and bound by Toppan Leefung Printing Ltd, China

www.pavilionbooks.com

60 Classic Indoor Games

Katie Hewett

COLLINS & BROWN

Contents

Introduction

In an age where you can even play games on your mobile phone, traditional indoor games, or parlour games as the Victorians called them, could be regarded as a thing of the past. However, I think there are many reasons for us to bring them back into the mainstream.

I grew up in the 1970s, some of it in Jersey in the Channel Islands, where television programmes didn't even begin until 4p.m. I also spent two weeks of the year with my grandparents in south-west Ireland and their tiny portable television was stowed away in a cupboard until the evening news started at 6p.m. Here, in spite of the beautiful countryside and glorious beaches, we tended to spend a great deal of time inside because it rained – a lot. Hence my fondness for indoor games (and endless fudge- and toffee-making – but perhaps that's for another book).

Indoor games work because they are simple, cost virtually nothing, require very little equipment, exercise the mind creatively and intellectually, and cut across generations – I can remember crying with laughter while playing a game of Consequences with my grandmother – but, most of all, because they are fun.

This book contains everything you need to play over 65 games, divided into sections depending on what sort of mood you are in: silly, energetic, clever, dramatic or quiet. There are games for the whole family to play together, games for mums and dads (and their friends), as well as children's games that most of us should remember, even if the rules are a little fuzzy around the edges.

Over the last few winters, heavy snowfalls have meant that thousands of children have been forced to stay at home for days at a time. So, once the snowmen have been built and the socks and gloves are drying on the radiator, rather than reach for the remote control why not play a few of these parlour games instead?

Silly Games

These are the games you play to get everyone in the mood, to cast off inhibitions and get the party started. When played by a group of people who know each other less well, they can be great ice-breakers.

Goodies and Baddies

Play time!
5 mins

Everyone loves playing keepie uppie with a balloon – however, this game has an exciting twist.

Stuff to Find
• An even number of players.
• A lot of balloons.

House Rules
Divide the players into two teams, the Goodies and the Baddies. The Goodies are given the blown-up balloon and it is their job to keep it airborne, while the Baddies have to try to burst it. The use of sharp objects, tackling or similar moves is not allowed.

When the Baddies have succeeded in bursting the balloon, the teams swap over their roles and start again with a second balloon.

The Picture Frame Game

Play time!
2 mins

A straight face is essential for this game – and if you've heard my son giggle then you will know how hard this can be!

Stuff to Find
• Two or more players.
• An empty picture frame or a frame made out of cardboard.

House Rules
The players make a circle and take it in turns to sit in the middle holding the picture frame. They have to hold the picture frame in front of their face, which must remain completely expressionless, for two minutes. If they move, twitch or laugh, they are out and must perform a forfeit. Play then passes to the next person.

Fun Forfeits

Games can be made even sillier by asking the players to perform forfeits if they lose a life or are disqualified. Here are some suggestions:

1. Recite the alphabet backwards.
2. Act like a chimpanzee.
3. Frown for one minute.
4. Skip 10 times with a skipping rope.
5. Wearing a blindfold, identify two people by touching their faces.
6. Recite a poem of your choice.
7. Have someone apply lipstick to you while blindfolded.
8. Swap socks with the person on your left.
9. Name 10 things you would find in the kitchen.
10. Wear a hat for the rest of the game.
11. Hug a person wearing glasses.
12. Pat your head with one hand, while rubbing your tummy with the other, for 30 seconds.
13. Do the opposite of three things ordered by other players.
14. Yawn until you make someone else yawn.
15. You are shipwrecked on an island inhabited by cannibals – explain to the chief why they shouldn't eat you.

Mummies

Tell the boys not to worry; no dolls are required for this game, just toilet roll and lots of laughter.

Stuff to Find
• An even number of players.
• A roll of toilet paper for each pair.

House Rules
Divide the players into pairs and give each team a roll of toilet paper. One member of the team then has three minutes to wrap their partner up in paper from head to foot so that they look like an Egyptian mummy. When the time is up, the team with the best mummy is the winner.

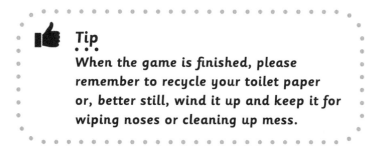

Tip

When the game is finished, please remember to recycle your toilet paper or, better still, wind it up and keep it for wiping noses or cleaning up mess.

Light and Shade

Play time! **20** mins

This game reminds me of shadow theatre. How will you hide your true identity from the audience?

Stuff to Find
• Six or more players.
• A white sheet.
• A lamp or torch.

House Rules
Hang the sheet across the room – a length of washing line and clothes pegs is probably the best way – and set up a lamp or shine a torch behind it.

Divide the players into two teams; members of the first team walk behind the sheet one at a time so their shadows are visible to the opposing team. This team then tries to guess the identity of the person behind the sheet – who is doing their best to disguise their silhouette. The team guessing gets two attempts per shadow and scores a point for each correct guess. Then the other team has their turn.

At the end of the game, the team with the most points wins.

Things Grandmas Say

'Don't pull that face: the wind will change
and it will stay that way.'

Blindfold Drawing

However talented you are at drawing, a blindfold creates a level playing field where art is concerned – as well as some hilarious pictures.

Stuff to Find
• Two or more players.
• A blindfold, some paper and a pencil for each player.

House Rules
Make sure all the players have a piece of paper and a pencil and are securely blindfolded. Then tell them what to draw. For example, start with their house, then ask them to add some trees in the garden, a car, some people, and so on – you can be as inventive as you like.

When the pictures are finished, everyone removes their blindfolds to see what they have drawn. There are no winners here – the laughter is the prize.

Kangaroo Racing

Play time!

5 mins

Everyone loves a balloon race. It is best to use your largest room for this game – or even the hallway if there is more space.

Stuff to Find
• Two or more players.
• One balloon for each player.

House Rules
First decide on a course and designate start and finish lines. Line all the players up at the start with their balloons between their knees; on the signal 'Go', they must start to jump down the course like kangaroos, being careful not to drop the balloon as they go. Any player who drops their balloon must catch it, put it back between their knees, and restart the race from the place they first dropped their balloon.

The first player to reach the finish line with their balloon intact is the winner. Anyone who bursts their balloon is instantly disqualified.

Deadpan

Play time!

10 mins

I love thinking of what to do next for this game. Most of the time, though, I only have to look as if I am going to tickle someone and my kids collapse into giggles.

Stuff to Find
• Four or more players.

House Rules
Everyone must sit on the floor in a circle as close together as possible. Choose a leader and then the game can start.

The leader nudges the person on their left and so on around the circle. When the nudge comes back to the leader, they then tweak the ear of the person on their left, and so on around the circle as before. Next time the leader can pull their neighbour's nose, tickle their ear, mess up their hair – basically anything to try to make them laugh. Speed is the name of the game. Anyone who even smiles – let alone giggles or laughs – is disqualified and must leave the circle.

Feelers

Play time!

20 mins

I used to play this at parties when I was young: anything slimy would have me running for the door!

Stuff to Find
- Three or more players.
- A pencil and some paper for each player.
- A pillowcase filled with assorted objects – 10 should be enough.

House Rules
Fill a pillowcase with an assortment of objects. The best ones to choose are items that could be mistaken for something else – for example, a grapefruit could also be a large orange, or a coin could be mistaken for another of a different value, etc.

Pass the pillowcase around, allowing each player 30 seconds to have a good feel before writing down as many of the objects they think they can identify. The player with the most accurate list is the winner.

Noises Off

Play time!

15
mins

You can let your imagination run away with you when preparing for this game – the more inventive the better, and the more fun everyone will have.

Stuff to Find
- Three or more players.
- Some paper and a pencil for each player.
- Everything you need to make some confusing and outrageous noises.

Noisy Suggestions
- Gargling
- Kissing
- Chalk on a blackboard
- Finger clicking

- Dropping a pin
- Cracking an egg
- Bouncing a ball
- Striking a match

House Rules

This game is probably better if it is organised in advance – then you can get together a whole range of unusual sounds.

The person making the noises must go behind a door or screen so they cannot be seen by the other players. They then make a succession of sounds that the other players have to guess and write down. The player that recognises the most sounds is the winner.

Musical Hats

Play time!

10 mins

This game is more sedate than musical bumps or statues and so better for a mixture of old and young and everyone in between – I like to use the silliest hats I can find.

Stuff to Find
• Four or more players.
• Hats for all players apart from one.

House Rules
The players sit in a circle, and all but one has a hat – they can be party paper hats or real hats depending on what is available.

When the music starts, the players pass the hats around the circle. When the music stops, all those with hats must put them on. The player without a hat leaves the circle and takes a hat with them. The game continues until only one player is left, and that person is the winner.

Squeak Piggy Squeak!

Play time! 20 mins

Remember, the sillier the squeak, the harder it is for the farmer to guess who you are!

Stuff to Find
• Five or more players.
• A blindfold and a cushion.

House Rules
Choose one player to be the 'farmer' and the others are the 'piggies'. The piggies sit down in a circle while the farmer is blindfolded and stands in the middle. Spin the farmer three times; they must then find their way, with their cushion, to one of the piggies and sit on their lap without touching the piggy with their hands. The farmer now says 'Squeak Piggy Squeak'; the chosen piggy must squeak and the farmer guesses the name of the player they are sitting on. If the farmer guesses correctly, the piggy is the farmer for the next round. If the farmer gets it wrong, then they stay to be spun again. It is a good idea for the piggies to change places before the next round begins.

Quiz Time
History

History was my favourite subject at school. Inspired by my teacher, who flew a Spitfire in World War II and told us his flight plans were written on rice paper so he could eat them if he was captured, I was hooked from the age of 10! Now it's your turn.

1. What is the name of the illustrated record of the Battle of Hastings in 1066?
2. Which city was believed to be founded in 753 BC?
3. Which treaty brought a formal end to World War I?
4. Which Ancient Greek physician is known as 'The father of modern medicine'?
5. Which monarch was executed in the English Civil War (1642–1651)?
6. Who made his first major voyage of discovery in 1492?
7. What does the 'D' stand for in Franklin D. Roosevelt?
8. How many of Henry VIII's wives were called Catherine?
9. The Crimean War (1853–1856) was fought by Britain and France against which other country?
10. Which country was divided by the 38th parallel after World War II?

Check the answers on pages 126–127.

Dramatic Games

Most of us enjoy the opportunity
to channel our inner thespian — whether
it is through mime, comedy, drama or
just plain over-acting. It is also a great
way to build the confidence of younger
members of the family.

Murder in the Dark

Play time!

20 mins

Played in the dark, this detective game is especially atmospheric. It is also good practice for anyone who has always longed to be Hercule Poirot for the evening.

Stuff to Find

• Six or more players.

• Pack of cards, or some paper, a pencil and a bowl or hat, and a house with lots of hiding places!

House Rules

If you are playing with a pack of cards, find the following: Ace, Jack, Queen, King and number cards for the remaining players. Give a card to each person. The player with the Ace is the murderer and the person holding the Jack is the detective. The King becomes the detective if the Jack is murdered, and the Queen becomes the detective if both the Jack and King are murdered.

If you are playing with pencil and paper, tear the paper into as many pieces as there are players. Mark a cross on one piece and a circle on another. The rest of the pieces stay blank. Fold up the paper slips and put them in a hat or bowl. Each player then picks one. The player that chooses the cross is the murderer and the person with the circle is the detective.

Before the game starts, the detective identifies him- or herself. Turn off the lights, and everyone find a place to hide. The murderer then finds a 'victim', touches them on the shoulder and whispers 'You're dead'. The player falls to the floor while letting out a bloodcurdling scream as the murderer creeps away.

When the players hear the scream, they must stay where they are. The detective then needs to go to the crime scene and switch on the lights, noting where everyone is. Now the detective calls everyone into the main room and asks the suspects a series of questions. Those that are innocent must tell the truth but the murderer can lie unless they are asked directly whether or not they are guilty. Once all the evidence has been collected, the detective then has two chances to guess the identity of the murderer.

Things Mums Say
• • • • • • • • • • • • •
'Put that down! You don't know
where it's been!'

I Have Never

I Have Never – had a filling in my adult teeth. I wonder how many people reading this can say that...

Stuff to Find
• Three or more players.

House Rules
Each player takes it in turn to declare something that they have never done. For example, you might say, 'I have never had a school meal'. If you turn out to be the only person that has never had a school meal, then you score a point, and the first person to gain three points wins the game.

 Tip
To increase your chance of scoring a point, think really carefully about things that at least one of the other players is likely to have done, or if you are being really cunning, try to think of something you know they have done and you haven't.

Going Blank

The faster the question master, the harder this game becomes, so think 'University Challenge' rather than 'Who Wants to be a Millionaire?'

Stuff to Find

• Four or more players.

House Rules

The players choose one person to be the question master who must then decide on three categories for questions, for example, the names of big cats, flowers and footballers. The players then stand or sit in a circle around the question master who points at a player before demanding an instant answer to each question.

During each round, the question master must ask each player three questions from each of the three categories but can do so in any order. If a player hesitates or gets the answer wrong, they are out. The winners are those remaining in the game when they have been asked three questions.

In the Manner of the Word

Play time!

5 mins per round

Also known as Adverbs, this game dates from the nineteenth century, and is a great way to teach a valuable grammatical tool without anyone noticing or using the words 'It's not fair'!

Stuff to Find
• Four or more people.

House Rules
There are two versions of this game. In either version, if you are able to guess the adverb you win the round, but with this game no one really cares.

Individuals

One person leaves the room and those remaining choose an adverb – for example, 'aggressively', 'wearily', 'excitedly', and so on. When the choice has been made, the person is called back into the room and they have to guess what the adverb is. They can do this either by asking questions that the other players have to answer 'in the manner of the word', or they can ask the player to act out an everyday situation, such as cleaning the windows or driving a car, also 'in the manner of the word'.

Pairs
In this version, two people go out of the room to think of an adverb. When they return, the others have to guess what it is by giving the pair situations to act out – you've guessed it – 'in the manner of the word'. Perhaps milking a cow, washing their hair, cutting the grass, etc.

Tips
- **More common adverbs are easier for younger players to manage.**
- **The second version is better suited to players with more inhibitions – they get to share the embarrassment!**

Wink Murder

I was never very good at screaming (see Murder in the Dark, pages 28–29), so pretending to die in an over-dramatic way was much more my thing.

Stuff to Find
• Four or more players.
• A pack of cards.

House Rules
Draw as many cards from the pack as there are players – one of these cards must be the Ace of Spades. Lay the cards on the table, and ask each player to pick a card, keeping its identity secret. The person with the Ace of Spades is the 'murderer'.

Sit everyone in a circle. Once the murderer has caught someone's eye, they wink in their direction and this player must slump forward and 'die'. The idea is for the murderer to kill everyone without their identity being discovered. If any of the players spot the murderer, then the game begins again.

Acting Proverbs

Play time!

5–10
mins per
round

Even though children may not know all the sayings,
this is a team game, so it is easy to get them involved.

Stuff to Find
· Six or more players.

House Rules
Divide the players into teams of three or four. One team must
go out of the room to think of a well-known proverb or saying
to act out for the other team to guess. They then come back
into the room and act out their choice in one scene. If the
other team guesses correctly, then it is their turn. If they are
unable to guess, then the acting team has another go.

Proverb Suggestions
· A stitch in time saves nine.
· Too many cooks spoil the broth.
· A rolling stone gathers no moss.

Charades

Charades is already a great favourite in my house. However, I am getting slightly weary of having to guess 'The Princess and the Frog' for the umpteenth time, and am looking forward to seeing the mime for 'Harry Potter and the Half-blood Prince' instead!

Stuff to Find
· Four or more people.

House Rules
Charades can be played in teams or as individuals. The idea is to act out the name of a well-known book, film, play, song, television programme, person or even a familiar saying, using a combination of actions and mime – speaking at any time is against the rules and will result in immediate disqualification.

If you are playing as individuals, one person acts out their choice and everyone else must try to guess what it is. The person that guesses correctly wins a point. If no one gets it, the person acting gets the point.

If you are playing in teams, you need to decide which team starts and within that team which member goes first. That team member acts out their choice to their own team who scores a point if they guess correctly. If they can't guess it then it, goes over to the other team who can score a bonus point if they can get it right.

Once you have mimed the category your choice is from, you can indicate the number of words it contains by holding up the relevant number of fingers: first word, second word, third word, etc.

Categories
. . . .

Book put your hands together and open them like a book.

Film pretend to be winding an old-fashioned movie camera.

Play put your hands together in front of you and move them downwards and apart to indicate curtains in a theatre.

Song bring a hand to your open mouth and then move it away to indicate sound.

Television programme draw a square in the air using two hands.

Saying use the index and middle finger of each hand to indicate quotation marks.

Some words are easy to act out, for instance, you can point to objects or people around the room. However, there are some other useful actions that can help with other words:

Useful Actions
. . . .

Small word holding your thumb and index finger a short distance apart indicates a small word. The other players must then shout out common small words, 'in', 'of', 'at', 'on', 'to', 'a', and you point to the first person to get it right.

The is indicated by making a letter 'T' with the index fingers of both hands.

Sounds like pinching your ear lobe is a way of showing that the word you want the players to guess 'sounds like' a word that is easier to act out.

Syllables you can also break a word up into syllables to make it easier to create the word. The action for this is to place the relevant number of fingers on the underside of your opposite forearm. For instance, if you had decided on the book 'To Kill a Mockingbird', you could break the last word up into three syllables.

Whole thing you can choose to act out the whole title; the action for this is to draw a circle in the air with both arms.

Dumb Crambo

Play time!

15 mins per round

The spoken version of this game – Crambo – is an old rhyming game that has been played for hundreds of years. In this game, only one word needs to be spoken in each round – hence the name 'Dumb' Crambo.

Stuff to Find

• Six or more people.

House Rules

Divide the players into two teams. One team leaves the room while the other team thinks of a word. When the first team is called back, they are not told the actual word chosen but another word that rhymes with it (for example, if the team had chosen the word 'bite', the word they give to the opposing team might be 'night').

The team that is guessing must then leave the room to think of three words that rhyme with 'night' that could be the correct answer. However, rather than return to the room and ask their opponents which of the words is correct, they must act out their guesses one by one. When the guesses are incorrect, the first team has the chance to boo and hiss to show their displeasure, but, if the answer is right, then this must be greeted with a great round of applause.

Variation
· · · · · · · ·

In the spoken version of this game, the team guessing can ask questions to find out what the word is. As above, they are given a word that rhymes with the word they are guessing, and they are allowed three chances to guess correctly, but cannot ask direct questions. Instead, they must ask indirect questions, for example:

- Is it something you turn on using a switch [a light – incorrect]?
- Is it something that might happen when two people get into an argument [a fight – incorrect]?
- Is it something you might get from a mosquito [a bite – correct]?

Coffee Pot

Play time!

5 mins per round

This game can be adapted for all ages and is guaranteed to create a lot of laughter.

Stuff to Find

• Between four and eight players.

House Rules

The idea is for one player to leave the room while the others think of a verb. When the first player returns, they can ask questions to find out what the chosen verb is but must use the words 'coffee pot' when asking the questions. An easy example would be:

Player 1: Where can you coffee pot?
Player 2: You can coffee pot at the sports centre.
Player 1: What do you need to coffee pot?
Player 3: You need a swimming costume and goggles.

So the verb is obviously 'to swim'. When the answer is guessed correctly, the next player takes their turn, and so on.

Throwing Smiles

This game takes a lot of self-control. You might think it sounds easy but let's see how quickly you lose your poker face!

Stuff to Find
• Four or more players.

House Rules
Everyone sits in a circle making sure all the players can see each other. Choose someone to be 'It' and they start the game. 'It' must then start to smile while everyone else must look serious. 'It' then uses their hand to wipe the smile off their face and throw it to another player who must catch it and put it on. The new 'It' must then smile broadly at all the other players before choosing someone to pass the smile on to.

Remember, only the person who is 'It' is allowed to smile, all the other players must look serious or they are out! If you are out, you are allowed to try to make the ones left in smile – but funny faces only, no tickling! The last serious person left in is the winner.

Quiz Time
Science and Nature

Biology, Chemistry, Maths – even double Maths – did not fill me with dread when I was at school. Physics, on the other hand, was another matter and I couldn't wait to give it up. Which of the sciences was your bête noire? Here are a few questions that might help you remember...

1. Diamonds are a form of which chemical element?
2. What is the longest bone in the human body?
3. Relating to flat-screen televisions and monitors, what does LCD stand for?
4. What is the mathematical series that starts 0,1,1,2,3,5,8,13,21 called?
5. Which sub-atomic particles are found in the nucleus of an atom?
6. Which sugar is found in milk?
7. Which is the largest species of big cat in South America?
8. What did Wilhelm Conrad Röntgen discover by accident on 8 November 1895?
9. In trigonometry, what is calculated by the adjacent over the hypotenuse?
10. What is the usual colour of copper sulphate?

Check the answers on pages 126–127.

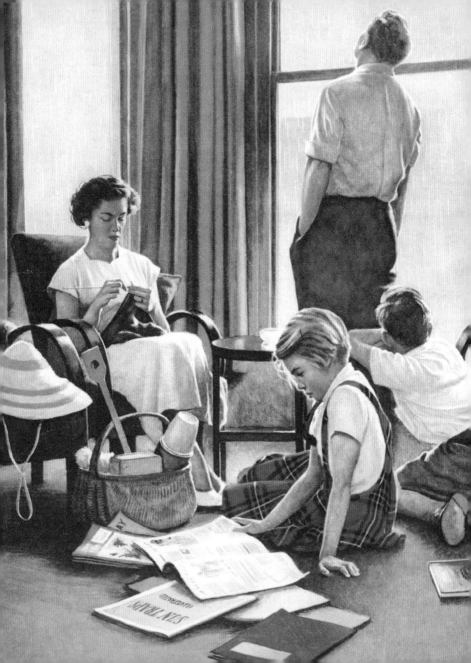

Pencil and Paper Games

Whether you are at home, on the train, at the airport or waiting at the doctor's surgery, all you need to play a huge variety of games is a pencil and a few scraps of paper.

Consequences

Guaranteed to produce both hysterical laughter and some of the most unlikely couples since Arthur Miller and Marilyn Monroe, this game works for all age groups and across generations.

Stuff to Find
- Two or more people.
- A pencil to share or one each and lots of paper – once you start you'll want to keep going!

House Rules
The aim of this game is to produce a hilarious short story by taking turns to write the different stages of the story without the other players knowing what you have written.

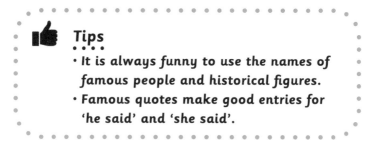

Tips
- It is always funny to use the names of famous people and historical figures.
- Famous quotes make good entries for 'he said' and 'she said'.

Choose someone to start and, using one piece of paper, begin the story by writing at the top. Once you have finished, you must fold the paper over so what is written cannot be seen, and pass it to the next player.

A number of different versions of the story formula exist but most include the following:

1. [Boy's name] met
2. [Girl's name] at
3. [Where they met]
4. He did [what he did]
5. She did [what she did]
6. He said [what he said to her]
7. She said [what she said to him]
8. And the consequence was [describe the consequence]
9. And the world said [what the world said].

Variation
• • • • • • • •
Alternatively, and this works better with a larger group of people, you can play a version where everyone has a piece of paper and a pencil and starts at the beginning. Once the first stage has been written, pass the paper to the player on your right.

Beetle

This game is down to the luck of the dice, and you don't need to be a great artist to play so everyone can join in.

Stuff to Find
• Between two and eight people.
• One dice and a piece of paper and a pencil for each player.

House Rules
The parts of the beetle are numbered to correspond with the numbers on the dice:

• 1 = body
• 2 = head
• 3 = tail
• 4 = eyes
• 5 = feelers
• 6 = legs

Taking it in turns, the object of the game is to throw the dice until you have a complete beetle. A finished beetle must have a body, a head, a tail, two eyes, two feelers and six legs.

Remember, you must throw a one (for a body) to start – if you don't, play passes to your left. You can't add eyes or feelers until you have a head (a two).

The first player to complete a beetle shouts 'Beetle' and wins the game.

Boxes

A great game of skill and strategy, Boxes is a good way to pass the time wherever you are. It can be surprisingly difficult, though, so don't get too frustrated and watch out for sibling arguments!

Stuff to Find
• Two people.
• Some paper and pens of two different colours to avoid disagreements.

House Rules
Mark out a grid using the same number of dots horizontally and vertically – 10 in each direction is about right for a 10-minute game.

Each using a different colour, you and your partner must take it in turns to draw a line between any two dots on the grid, in an attempt to make a box. When you complete a box, you can mark it with your initial and then draw another line and so on. If the line encloses another box you mark it too.

When all the boxes have been completed, the game is over and you must count up your boxes to see who has the most – that person is the winner.

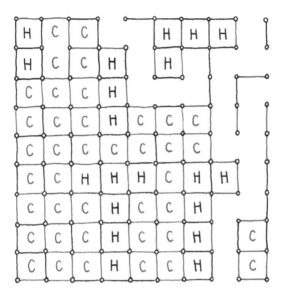

Variation
. . . .
For a change, you can always play the game with the reverse approach – so the person with the fewest boxes wins.

Sprouts

Play time!

5 mins

Sprouts is a fiendish brain tease.

Stuff to Find
• Two players.
• Some paper and two pencils (different colours if possible).

House Rules
Draw eight dots spaced out on a piece of paper. The first person then draws a line joining any two dots, or joining a dot to itself, then draws a dot somewhere along the new line. The next person does the same. There are three rules that determine whether a line is permissible:

• It must not cross either itself or any other line.
• It must not pass through a dot.
• No dot must have more than three lines leading from it.

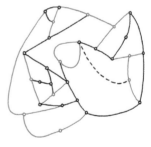

The winner is the player to draw the last permissible line.

Noughts and Crosses

Known in the US as Tic-tac-toe, this is a quick, addictive and competitive game.

Stuff to Find
• Two players.
• Some paper and a pencil.

House Rules
Draw a simple four-line grid creating nine spaces (three rows of three). One player is 'X' and the other '0'. Traditionally the person who is 'X' goes first but that is up to you!

The first player places their mark in one space in the grid, then the second player does the same. The aim of the game is to get three of your marks in a row, either horizontally, vertically or diagonally. The player that succeeds in doing this is the winner.

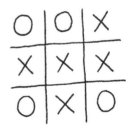

Anagrams

Play time!
30 mins

You can make this game as easy or as difficult as you like – you can challenge your crossword-wizard granny or help your younger ones with their spelling.

Stuff to Find
• Two players, or teams of equal numbers; a question master.
• A pencil and some paper.

House Rules
The question master decides on one or more categories (see above right). You can have as many as you like but five is usually enough for a 30-minute game. Then the question master prepares a list of words for each category, makes anagrams of the words and gives each player (or team) a copy.

The players are given a time limit to solve all the anagrams in each category, so, if you have five categories with three anagrams for each, for a 30-minute game the time limit for each category would be six minutes.

The player (or team) who solves the most anagrams in the time given is the winner.

Category Suggestions

- Films
- Mammals
- Pop stars
- Types of sport
- Capital cities
- Famous authors
- Food
- Makes of car
- Book titles
- Body parts
- Famous artists
- Hobbies

Variation

If two people want to play but there is no one to be the question master, decide on the categories together and devise an agreed number of anagrams for each category. You can then swap over your anagrams and the first person to solve them all is the winner.

Battleships

Play time!
15 mins

Your grandad will prefer the traditional version of this game but you can choose any vessels you like – starships, pirate ships, army vehicles – it's up to you.

Stuff to Find
• Two players.
• A pencil and some paper.

House Rules
Each player needs to draw two grids 10 squares by 10 squares, numbered from one to 10 down the left-hand side and from A to J across the top. One grid is for the home fleet and the other is for the enemy fleet. Each player's fleet consists of:

• One battleship (four squares marked with a 'B')
• Two cruisers (three squares each marked with a 'C')
• Three destroyers (two squares each marked with a 'D')
• Four submarines (one square marked with an 'S').

Mark your ships on your home fleet grid. The squares that make up each ship must touch one another horizontally, vertically or diagonally and no two ships should touch.

Toss a coin to decide who starts and then the players take turns to try to hit the enemy fleet. You do this by calling out the reference for the square (for example, 'C6', 'A8'). All direct hits must be declared by the enemy and the type of vessel given honestly. You can mark your hits and misses on your enemy fleet grid and plot your progress.

The winner is the first player to destroy the enemy fleet.

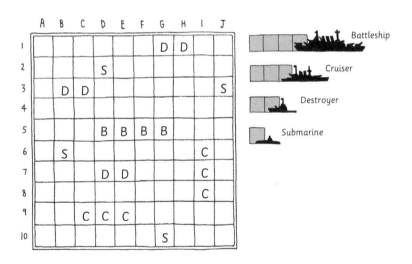

Alphabet Race

A homemade version of a very famous game, but no less of a challenge. You can make your own rules to cater for everyone in your family.

Stuff to Find
- Two or more players.
- A pencil, one piece of paper for each player and a large piece of paper to be the board.

House Rules
Before the game begins, each player must list the letters of the alphabet on their piece of paper. On the larger piece of paper draw a grid 10 squares by 10 squares. Toss a coin to see who will start.

The first player writes down a word on the piece of paper being used as the board (make sure the letters are spaced out carefully) either vertically or horizontally, then they cross off those letters on their own alphabet list. The next player adds a word to the grid that intersects with the first word and crosses off the letters they have used on their alphabet list.

Letters can only be used once and if you are stuck you can 'pass' and play passes to the next person. The first player to use all their letters is the winner but it can be tricky, so you may prefer to set a time limit and see who has used the most letters at the end of the game.

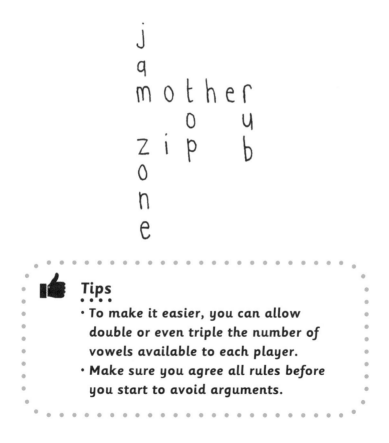

Tips

- To make it easier, you can allow double or even triple the number of vowels available to each player.
- Make sure you agree all rules before you start to avoid arguments.

The Name Game

Play time!

15–20 mins

This game is noisy, infuriating and hilarious.

Stuff to Find
• Four or more players – larger teams make it more fun.
• Pencils, pieces of paper and a bowl to put the names in.

House Rules
Divide the players into two teams, and everyone writes the names of up to 10 famous people on separate slips of paper – alive or dead, film stars, television personalities, athletes, etc. Fold the slips and put them in the bowl. Toss a coin to decide which team goes first and decide how long each round will last.

For each round, one person on each team must pick a slip from the bowl and describe the person on it. When the team has guessed correctly, the person describing picks out another name and keeps going until the round is over. When all the names have been used, the team that has guessed the most is the winner.

Wordbuilder

Play time!

10
mins

This is a basic version of the commercial game Boggle.

Stuff to Find
• Two or more players.
• Some paper and a pencil for each player.

House Rules
Choose a word to start with, preferably a long one. Each player then writes this on a piece of paper. You then have 10 minutes to make as many words as you can from the letters of the chosen word. The person who makes the most words is the winner. You can vary the rules according to who is playing but some good ones include:

• Each word must contain at least four letters.
• Proper nouns are not allowed.
• Words from other languages, abbreviations and plurals are not allowed.
• A letter may only be used in a word as many times as it appears in the starter word.

Quiz Time
Geography

Geography got a bad rap when I was at school: the teachers wore brown suits, we didn't care what an ox-bow lake was, and what was a tertiary industry?

However, to even the score, here are some really good questions on geography and travel – how many do you know?

1. Which island group includes Ibiza, Menorca and Majorca?
2. The ancient city of Machu Picchu is in which country?
3. Dulles International Airport serves which American city?
4. On which river are the Victoria Falls found?
5. Which landlocked sea is 422m (1385ft) below sea level?
6. What is created when the loop of a meander of a river is cut off and the river diverted on a different course?
7. Of which republic are English, Malay, Mandarin Chinese and Tamil the four official languages?
8. Which country's flag includes a cedar tree?
9. Mauritius is found in which ocean?
10. Who developed the most-used projection for maps of the world in 1569?

Check the answers on pages 126–127.

Word Games

Guessing games, memory games, quick-thinking games, games with letters and games with numbers – there are so many games to play with nothing but your eyes, ears, mouths and minds. Who needs brain training?

Twenty Questions

Also known as 'Animal, Vegetable or Mineral?' this game is an old favourite. It is also a good way to make something educational feel like fun.

Stuff to Find
• Three or more people.

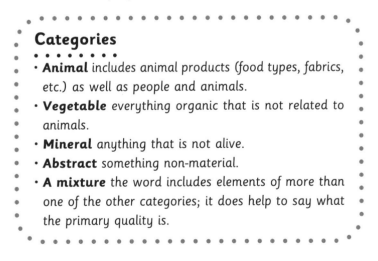

Categories
• **Animal** includes animal products (food types, fabrics, etc.) as well as people and animals.
• **Vegetable** everything organic that is not related to animals.
• **Mineral** anything that is not alive.
• **Abstract** something non-material.
• **A mixture** the word includes elements of more than one of the other categories; it does help to say what the primary quality is.

House Rules

In the traditional version, one player thinks of an object or concept and tells the others what category it is.

The players are allowed 20 questions that require Yes or No answers designed to limit the field and eventually close in on the word. You can make a direct challenge, 'Is it XX?', but, if you get the answer wrong, you are out of that round. The first player to guess correctly gets to choose the next word but, if no one guesses the answer the person who chose the word is the winner for that round and can choose again.

Variation
• • • • • • •
For a change, you can play the game the other way around: one player leaves the room and everyone else chooses a word. When they return, the person guessing gets 20 questions to try to work out the answer. This can be played as a knockout competition too: each player continues in the game until they fail to answer correctly. The last person left is the winner.

Word Association

Play time!

5 mins

The idea of this game is to build up a long chain of associated words; the faster it is played, the funnier it becomes.

Stuff to Find
· Three or more people.

House Rules
Choose someone to start who must say the first word that comes into their mind. The second player must come up with an associated word, followed by the third player and so on.

If you hesitate, you are out of the round. If your word is not obviously associated with the preceding word, another player can challenge you. If the other players accept your explanation, the game continues and the challenger loses a life. If they are not convinced, you lose a life. Once you have used up three lives, you must drop out. The person left in is the winner.

Number Association

This game gives you the chance to show off your knowledge of language, music and literature – you know you want to...

Stuff to Find
• Three or more people.

House Rules
Taking it in turns, each player calls out a number between 1 and 12. The first person to call out an appropriate association wins a point. There must be no repetition. When everyone has had enough, the person with the most points is the winner.

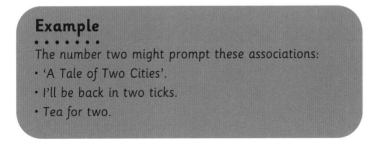

Example
• • • • • •
The number two might prompt these associations:
• 'A Tale of Two Cities'.
• I'll be back in two ticks.
• Tea for two.

I Love My Love

Play time!

10 mins

You've heard the expression 'Honesty is the best policy' but I'm not sure it applies to this game!

Stuff to Find

• Three or more people.

House Rules

Decide who is going to start and then, taking it in turns, each player completes the sentence 'I love my love because he/she is…' using adjectives that go through the alphabet from A to Z. For example:

Player 1: I love my love because she is Aggressive.
Player 2: I love my love because he is Balding.
Player 3: I love my love because she is Cranky.

You can obviously decide to give your loved one a ringing endorsement (whether they deserve it or not) but it is funnier to be rather less complimentary!

Any player who cannot come up with an adjective that begins with the appropriate letter is out of the game, and the last person left is the winner.

Variation
• • • • • • • •
For younger players, you might want to try a different version of this game called The Minister's Cat. Here, the first person starts by saying 'The Minister's cat is...' and has to think of an adjective to describe the cat beginning with 'a', for example, 'The Minister's cat is an angry cat'. The next person does the same but with the letter 'b' and so on around the group.

You can play this as a knockout game as above, but it could also be a group effort, with everyone helping out to see if you are able to find adjectives for all the letters of the alphabet.

Things Mums Say
• • • • • • • • • • • • •
'I didn't ask who put it there, I said,
"Pick it up!"'

Botticelli

Play time!

20 mins

This complex game used to be known as **The Box**, because the person questioned feels as if they are in the witness box.

Stuff to Find
• Three or more people.

House Rules
Player one thinks of a famous character – fictional or real, dead or alive. They then announce the first letter of the person's surname to the rest of the players. The players now have to think of someone whose name begins with that letter and, taking it in turns, they ask indirect questions about the famous character.

Player 1: My surname begins with 'D'.
Player 2: Do you solve mysteries?

Player one now has to think of a character whose surname begins with the same letter that answers the question. When they think of it, if it is incorrect, they tell the players it is not them and the next player asks another indirect question.

Player 1: No, I am not Scooby Doo.
Player 3: Are you famous for drawing a mouse?

If player one can't think of an answer, they tell the group. The player who asked the last question gives the answer and then asks a direct question and player one must answer with 'yes' or 'no'.

Player 1: I don't know.
Player 3: Walt Disney. Are you an actor?
Player 1: No.

Sometimes there is more than one answer to an indirect question, and player one may respond with one of the other answers.

Player 4: Are you a cartoon duck?
Player 1: No, I am not Daffy Duck.

But if this is a direct question they must confirm their identity.

Player 1: Yes, I am Donald Duck.

If no one guesses in 20 minutes, player one wins and announces their identity. If another player guesses, then that player becomes player one in the next round.

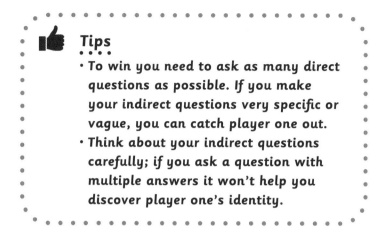

👍 **Tips**

- To win you need to ask as many direct questions as possible. If you make your indirect questions very specific or vague, you can catch player one out.
- Think about your indirect questions carefully; if you ask a question with multiple answers it won't help you discover player one's identity.

Wordsworth

Play time!
5 mins

This is easy to adapt for a mixed group – give younger players more common letters, while grown-ups can have the harder ones.

Stuff to Find
• Three or more players.
• Some paper and a pencil for each player.

House Rules
Choose a player to start and give them a letter of the alphabet. In one minute they must list as many nouns as they can that begin with that letter. This player then nominates someone else to go next and a letter of the alphabet, and so on until all the players have had a turn. The person who is able to think of the most nouns is the winner.

Make sure you decide as a group before play begins which letters are too tricky to be included, for example, X, Z and Q.

Buzz, Fizz, Fizz-Buzz

Play time!
5–10 mins

These three closely related games involve substituting words for numbers. As well as being fun, they can help younger ones learn their times-tables – and can help older players revise them!

Stuff to Find
• Two or more players.

House Rules
All three games begin in the same way. The players sit in a circle and the first person begins counting from 'one'. The faster the game is, the more fun it is – and the easier it is to make a mistake!

Buzz

In this version, every time you reach a number with a seven, or any multiple of seven, you must say 'Buzz'.

Fizz

If you are playing Fizz, you must use the word 'Fizz' when you reach a number with a five or any multiple of five.

Fizz-Buzz

Unsurprisingly, Fizz-Buzz is a combination of the two, and you must use either 'Fizz' or 'Buzz', or both at the same time (in the case of 35, 57, 70 and 75) at the appropriate time.

Any player who says a number instead of Fizzing or Buzzing, or who Fizzes when they should have Buzzed (or vice versa), is out of the game. The last player left in is the winner.

Variation
• • • • • • • •
To make the game harder, you can choose a smaller number with more multiples to be 'Fizz', like the number 'three'.

Things Grandpas Say
• • • • • • • • • • • • • • • •
'If a job is worth doing, it is worth doing well.'

The Yes/ No Game

Just how hard is it not to use the words 'yes' or 'no' under pressure? Why don't you find out?

Stuff to Find
- Two or more players.
- A watch to time the rounds.

House Rules
For this game, one person asks questions and another person answers. The person answering must not answer 'yes' or 'no' to any questions during the two-minute round. You can also ban words like 'er' and 'um' to make it harder.

Question Suggestions
- Are you ready?
- Are you sure you are ready?
- Right, shall we start?

I Packed My Bag

Play time!

10 mins

Also known as I Went To Market and Portmanteau (an old-fashioned word for a suitcase), I find my children are usually better at this memory game than I am!

Stuff to Find
• Two players or more.

House Rules
The first player starts the round with 'I packed my bag'. The next player then says 'I packed my bag and put in...' and adds an item. The player who goes next must say the item the previous player added to the bag, before adding their own item, and so on, with the list of items getting longer and longer as the game continues. If anyone omits an item, or places it in the incorrect order, that person is out of the round.

If you want to make the list slightly easier to remember, you can add the rule that the items should be added in alphabetical order.

Spelling Bees

Play time!

20 mins

Spelling tests are the bane of most schoolchildren's lives but spelling competitions have been fiercely fought since the first National Spelling Bee took place in America in 1911.

Stuff to Find
• Two players or two equal teams plus a question master.
• A dictionary.

House Rules
The question master calls out a word for the first player (or team) to spell. If they spell it correctly, they score one point. The second player (or team) is then given their word, and so on. If the word is spelled incorrectly, it is passed to the other player (or team) and, if they can spell it correctly, they score an extra point. At the end of the round (10 words per round is a good number), the player (or team) with the most points is the winner.

The question master may use words from a pre-prepared list or make up the list as they go along – take care to use words of equal difficulty or there will be arguments! To make the game harder, you can try spelling the words backwards.

Taboo

Play time!

20 mins

This game proves yet again that doing something very simple is actually very difficult – and we all know how much children like to make their parents look silly!

Stuff to Find
• Three or more people.

House Rules

Choose a word that comes up frequently in conversation, such as 'and', 'the' or 'it'; once everyone has agreed on the word it becomes 'taboo'. Then one person becomes the question master and asks the other players about anything at all in an attempt to make them say the forbidden word – anyone who does so, or hesitates, is out, and the last player left is the winner.

Variation
· · · · · · · ·
To make the game more difficult, you can make a letter of the alphabet taboo and any word containing it is also taboo. This version is only for experienced players!

Quiz Time
Entertainment

Many of us spend far more time at the cinema and watching television than we might care to admit, but it means we know a fair amount about popular culture.

1. Betty Draper is the wife, and Peggy Olsen is the advertising executive, from which acclaimed television series?
2. 'As far back as I can remember, I always wanted to be a gangster.' Ray Liotta said this in which film from 1990?
3. 'You Give Love a Bad Name' and 'Livin' on a Prayer' were early hits for which band?
4. What are the surnames of Romeo and Juliet?
5. 'Who loves ya, baby' was a catchphrase of which 1970s lollipop-sucking detective?
6. Who played Maximus Decimus Meridius in a 2000 Ridley Scott film?
7. What was Elvis Presley's middle name?
8. Despite the legend, in which film is 'Play it again, Sam' never actually said?
9. First performed in 1918, who composed The Planets suite?
10. In 2009, which band released the album 'West Ryder Pauper Lunatic Asylum'?

Check the answers on pages 126–127.

Action Games

If it's raining outside, it's good to find
ways to use up all that excess energy, so
here are a selection of games that can
help everyone blow off some steam.
Even Dad – if you can get him to come
out from behind the newspaper!

Tiddlywinks

Play time!

20 mins

Elevated from a parlour game played by children to an international sport, the game of Tiddlywinks was first patented in Britain in 1888 by Joseph Assheton Fincher. This simplified version is great for playing at home.

Stuff to Find
- Two to four people.
- A set of coloured counters for each player, each consisting of six smaller 'winks' and a larger 'squidger' used to flick the 'winks'.
- A rectangular piece of felt or other non-slip fabric.
- A plastic pot.

House Rules
Place each set of counters in a corner of the playing mat and the plastic pot in the centre. If two people are playing, they can use two sets each; in a team game, the team members should sit diagonally opposite one another, and play moves clockwise around the mat.

A 'squidge-off' decides who goes first: each player flicks or 'squidges' one wink as close to the pot as possible. The winner gets to go first. The aim is to get all your winks into the pot (to 'pot out'). If you pot a wink, you get an extra turn. If you shoot a wink off the mat, it must be returned to its original position and you miss a turn. If one wink lands on top of another, that wink becomes 'squopped' and neither of these winks can be played.

The game ends when you reach an agreed time limit, when a player pots out, or when there are no more playable winks on the mat. If no one pots out, you can count all the winks in the pot and the player (or team) with the most wins.

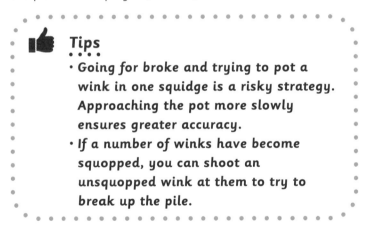

Tips

- Going for broke and trying to pot a wink in one squidge is a risky strategy. Approaching the pot more slowly ensures greater accuracy.
- If a number of winks have become squopped, you can shoot an unsquopped wink at them to try to break up the pile.

Things Mums Say
'Do as I say, not as I do.'

Pass the Orange

No hands are allowed for this game so it is a good thing that oranges are so resilient!

Stuff to Find
• Two teams, ideally six or more on each side.
• An orange for each team.

House Rules
Each team stands in a line and the first player in each tucks the orange under their chin. They then have to pass the orange to the next player without using their hands. When the orange reaches the end of the line, that player runs to the front of the line and the process begins again. Play continues until the first person returns to the front of the line. This team is the winner.

Things Grandmas Say
• • • • • • • • • • • • • • • •
'A bird in the hand is worth two in the bush.'

Paper, Scissors, Stone

Play time!

30 secs per round

Great fun for all ages even young children.

Stuff to Find
• Two players.

House Rules
Both players hold out one hand in a fist and count 'One, two, three' before each making one of the three signs below at the same time:
• Paper an open hand.
• Scissors index and middle fingers used to imitate scissors.
• Stone a clenched fist.

The outcomes are as follows:
• Stone blunts scissors stone defeats scissors.
• Scissors cut paper scissors defeats paper.
• Paper covers stone paper defeats stone.

This game is usually played as a 'best of three', but, if you both make the same sign, then that round is not counted.

Pop the Balloon

**I always say you can never have too many balloons —
they are the ultimate in low-tech entertainment.**

Stuff to Find

- Six or more people.
- At least two balloons for each player with string to attach
  them; for a team game each team will need a different colour.
- A music player and someone to operate it.

House Rules

Divide the players into two or more teams. Tie balloons to
each of the players' feet so that each person has two balloons.
When the music starts the players need to move around the
room, but when it stops they must try to burst the balloons
belonging to members of the opposing team, while trying
to protect their own balloons. The stomping stops when the
music starts again.

　If you lose both balloons, you are out. When the game ends,
the team with the most balloons intact wins.

Duck, Duck, Goose

Children love this game so it is a good opportunity for the grown-ups to have a well-earned rest.

Stuff to Find
• Five or more players.

House Rules
The players sit in a large circle facing inwards. One player is chosen to be 'It' (or the 'Fox') and walks around the outside of the circle. As the Fox walks around, they touch each player gently on the head saying 'Duck, Duck, Duck'. At some point the Fox will say 'Goose' instead of 'Duck'. The 'Goose' must then jump up and chase the Fox around the circle. The Fox must try to get all the way back to the Goose's place without getting caught.

If the Fox gets there safely, the Goose becomes the Fox and the game starts again. If the Goose catches the Fox, the same Fox must try to catch the next Goose.

Hunt the Thimble

My children love this. Sometimes I will hide their favourite toy instead, but not Buzz Lightyear – he is too big and inclined to talk and give the game away!

Stuff to Find

• Three or more people.
• A thimble or another small object.

House Rules

All the players except one go out of the room, while the one remaining 'hides' the thimble. It should not really be hidden but placed in plain sight somewhere inconspicuous so that it is not immediately noticeable.

The other players are then called back into the room and begin to hunt the thimble. As soon as a player spots it, they must sit down without saying anything or drawing attention to the place the thimble has been hidden. The last player to spot the thimble is the one who hides it for the next round.

Sardines

My uncle and aunt had a house that was great for sardines – with four floors, lots of staircases and even an old butler's pantry, we never ran out of different places to hide.

Stuff to Find
• Four or more players.

House Rules
Draw lots to decide who will hide first and how long they can have to find their hiding place – five minutes is probably sufficient. When the time is up, the rest of the players separate to hunt for them.

The first player to find the person that is hiding waits until everyone else is out of sight, and then jumps into the hiding place to wait for the next player to find them. This goes on until all but one of the players are hiding together – like sardines in a tin – and the last player becomes the next person to hide.

Are You There, Moriarty?

Play time!

1 min per round

This game was invented in the late nineteenth century when Sherlock Holmes and his nemesis Moriarty were all the rage. Make sure you have a referee – dads in particular can take games like this a bit too seriously!

Stuff to Find
• Two players, plus an audience.
• Two rolled-up newspapers.
• Two blindfolds.

House Rules
Each player is blindfolded and given a rolled-up newspaper to use as a 'weapon' – make sure the newspapers are strong enough to deal an accurate blow but not rigid enough to cause an injury! Flip a coin to see who will start.

The players must then lie down on their fronts opposite one another, head to head, about 1m (3ft) apart. The starting player says, 'Are you there, Moriarty?' and, when they are ready, the other player says 'Yes'. When the first player has heard where their opponent's voice is coming from, they then attempt to hit them on the head with the newspaper.

If the first player misses, their opponent is then given the opportunity to ask, 'Are you there, Moriarty?' and have their go at scoring a hit. The game continues until one of the players succeeds in hitting the other on the head. Two new players can now join the game – or you can play 'winner stays on' if you prefer.

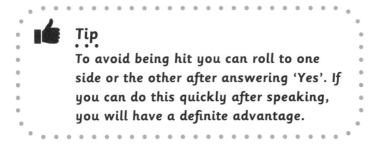

Tip

To avoid being hit you can roll to one side or the other after answering 'Yes'. If you can do this quickly after speaking, you will have a definite advantage.

Variation
• • • • • • •
You can also play this game standing up and holding opposite hands. Ducking and weaving will help you avoid being hit in this version.

Matchbox Race

This game is a great ice-breaker but perhaps not the best one to play with someone who has a cold!

Stuff to Find
· Six or more players.
· The sleeves of two matchboxes.

House Rules
Divide the players into two teams and ask each team to stand in line, one behind the other, with their hands held behind their backs.

   The first person in each line puts the matchbox sleeve on their nose, and when the order is given to 'Go' they must pass it to the next player using only their nose, and so on until the matchbox reaches the end of the line. If any player drops the matchbox, it is returned to the first person and the process must start all over again. The first team to get the matchbox to the end of the line wins.

Fish Flap

This is a perfect way to make good use of all those free newspapers that come through your front door.

Stuff to Find
• Three or more players.
• Some old newspapers.
• Scissors and a pen.

House Rules
Draw a basic fish shape, about 30cm (12in) long, onto the front of one of the newspapers. Cut around the shape through all layers and give a fish to each player. The players will also need a few sheets from a newspaper folded into a rectangle. This needs to be rigid to flap the 'fish' along the floor.

Designate starting and finishing lines, and at the signal 'Go' the players must flap their fish to the finish. The first one to the there is the winner.

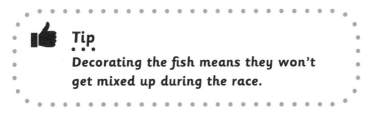

Tip
Decorating the fish means they won't get mixed up during the race.

Apple Bobbing

This game has been played for centuries – it is even depicted in some medieval paintings. Even though it is associated with Halloween, it is probably best played in warmer weather!

Stuff to Find
• Two or more players.
• A large bowl of water and some apples.

House Rules
Place a large bowl of water in the middle of a large space (make sure you also put down some plastic sheeting to protect the floor), and drop some apples into the water – usually one for every person taking part.

If you have enough room (and a big enough bowl), this game is most fun when everyone plays at the same time, but, to minimise the risk of potential flooding, you may decide to let the players take turns individually.

Kneeling on the floor, with your hands behind your back, the aim is to try to pick up the apples using only your mouth and teeth. You can tailor the rules to suit the way you have chosen to play.

- If you are all playing together, you can decide that for each round the first person to pick an apple right out of the bowl is the winner.
- If you are taking turns, you can set a time limit, say one minute, and see how many apples each player can pick out of the bowl during that time. The person who manages to pick out the most apples is the winner.

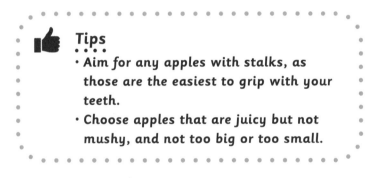

Tips
- Aim for any apples with stalks, as those are the easiest to grip with your teeth.
- Choose apples that are juicy but not mushy, and not too big or too small.

Things Grandpas Say

'An apple a day keeps the doctor away.'

Blind Man's Buff

Play time!

15 mins

This is another old game – there are even references to it being played in ancient China and at the court of King Henry VIII.

Stuff to Find
• Five or more players.
• A blindfold.

House Rules
One person is chosen to be 'It' and is blindfolded. They are then led to the centre of the room and turned around three times so they become slightly disorientated – but not so much that they fall over! The other players scatter around the room and the person who is blindfolded tries to catch them. When someone is caught, they are not allowed to move their feet but can twist around to try to escape. The blindfolded player now has to try to establish the identity of the person they have caught using touch alone. If they get it wrong, they have to let the player go. The last person to be caught is the winner.

Blow Football

You don't need a huge amount of skill for this game, just a lot of puff.

Stuff to Find
- Two or more players.
- A ping-pong ball or a cotton wool ball.
- Drinking straws.
- Small boxes.

House Rules
First of all, create your pitch by putting a border around the edge of the table to stop the ball falling off and placing a goal at each end – children's shoe boxes are good for this, but you could always just cut an old cereal box in half.

Start from the centre line, like regular football (toss a coin to see who goes first), and the idea is for the two opponents or teams to get the ball into the goal at the other end of the pitch, but rather than kicking the ball you blow it along using a straw. You can set a time limit or see which side is the first to reach 10 goals.

Quiz Time
Art and Literature

Everyone has a favourite novel, and, even if we might not like art, we always have an opinion about it – that's the point. Answer these 10 questions and see how cultured you are.

1. Which American abstract artist is best known for his 'drip paintings'?
2. The Bennet family appear in which Jane Austen novel?
3. Who created the famous sculptures 'The Thinker' and 'The Kiss'?
4. Who was the father of Goneril, Regan and Cordelia?
5. How are the sisters Meg, Jo, Beth and Amy described in the title of an 1868 novel?
6. Who painted 'The Laughing Cavalier'?
7. Which literary characters set out on a journey from the Tabard Inn, Southwark, in London?
8. Who is the Greek Goddess of Love?
9. The Meissen factory in Germany was one of the first manufacturers of which type of ceramic?
10. Who wrote the 'Twilight' series of novels?

Check the answers on pages 126–127.

Quiet Games

There's only so much romping around we can take, so here are some quieter games to play when you need to calm everyone down and give yourself the chance to tidy up — or have a rest!

Hangman

Play time!

10 mins

This works well as a game for two slightly older children playing together, but at the moment my two play as a team against me so they can help each other out.

Stuff to Find
• Two players.
• Some paper and a pencil.

House Rules
The first player thinks of a word and draws a row of dashes to represent each letter of the word. The second player then needs to guess the letters in the word. If they guess a letter that does occur, the first player writes it in where it appears (this may be more than once). If the suggested letter does not appear, the first player draws one element of the hangman diagram instead.

Features of the diagram vary depending on where you learned to play this game. The version I know contained 12 elements, as seen opposite. This means you can suggest up to 11 incorrect letters before you lose the game.

The game is over when the word is completed or guessed correctly or the first player completes the hangman diagram.

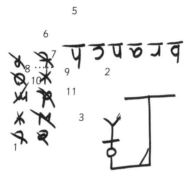

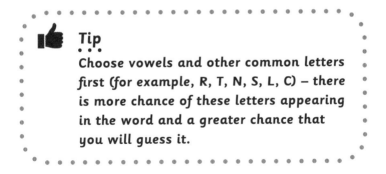

The Memory Game

This game first appeared in the novel 'Kim' by Rudyard Kipling and is also known as Kim's Game. It has since been adopted by the Scouting movement and by the military to help develop observational skills.

Stuff to Find
- Between two and eight players.
- A tray of household items (cup, saucer, ball of string, pen, etc.), a cloth to cover it up, plus a piece of paper and a pen for each player.

House Rules
Put the tray where all the players can see it. Uncover the items (about 12 items is a good number) and let the players memorise them for one minute. Cover the tray up again and then give the players two minutes to write down as many items as they can remember. The winner is the player who remembers the most items correctly.

I Spy

Fun for children but quite tedious for adults after about two minutes! My daughter catches me out in the middle of a game by choosing abstract things like 'spots'.

Stuff to Find
• Two or more players.

House Rules
One player selects an object in the room and says 'I spy with my little eye, something beginning with...' followed by the first letter of the chosen object. The person or people guessing then try to name all the objects beginning with that letter and the first person to get it right is the winner and chooses the object for the next round.

Variation
• • • • • • •
Chatty pre-school children like this game too but may not yet know their alphabet. Instead of letters you can choose objects by their colour or shape.

Dictionary Game

Play time!
30 mins

As this is a team game, even younger players can join in and will enjoy trying to outwit the other team.

Stuff to Find
- Between four and six players (two teams of three is best).
- Paper, pencils and a good dictionary.

House Rules
The players split into two teams and each team picks an unusual word from the dictionary. One member of each team writes down the real meaning of the word, while the other two make up entertaining, convincing but ultimately false definitions of the same word.

The members of the first team then present their definitions to the opposing team who have to decide which is the correct one. If they guess correctly, they win a point. Then the second team takes its turn.

You can continue for as many rounds as you wish and at the end the team with the most points is the winner.

Tips

- Make sure you have a good dictionary or you won't find many words that are sufficiently obscure.
- When presenting a false definition, if you relate it to a subject you know a lot about, such as technology, you will be at your most convincing, and have a better chance of fooling your opponents.

Things Mums Say

'Don't sit too close to the television – you'll get square eyes.'

Track Record

In my family we don't have that many secrets, so this game works better with friends and extended family that can still surprise us.

Stuff to Find
• At least six players.
• Pens and paper.

House Rules
Divide the players into two teams of three, and within each team each player must think of a strange, amusing or unlikely thing that has happened to them in the past. The chosen thing must be true.

These short anecdotes are written down anonymously and passed in a hat to the opposing team. This team then takes it in turn to read out the three anecdotes and must decide which member of the other team each applies to. Points are awarded for each correct guess, so the highest score wins.

Who Said That?

Play time!
20 mins

For this game it helps if you know the other players well – both how people say things and how much they know about you.

Stuff to Find
• At least six players.
• Pens and paper.

House Rules

One person leaves the room while the others write down an amusing or perceptive observation about them. The group then chooses the best three statements and invites the first player back into the room.

The best three statements are read out and the first player must try to guess who wrote them. One point is given for each correct guess. The player with the most points at the end of the game is the winner.

Stairway

This is a clever word-building game that really tests your word power. Don't forget to find a dictionary to settle disagreements.

Stuff to Find
· Two or more players.
· Paper and pencils.

House Rules
Make sure each player has a piece of paper and a pencil, and then choose a letter at random. Players have a set amount of time – 5 to 10 minutes is about right – to build as long a stairway as possible, in which each word begins with the chosen letter and each subsequent word is one letter longer than the one before.

The winner is the player with the longest list when the time is up; but remember, if you make a spelling mistake, you will be disqualified.

Transformation

Play time!

10 mins

This game can be adapted for all ages and helps to keep everyone's mind agile, especially when the words start to get a bit longer.

Stuff to Find
• Three or more players.
• Paper and pencils.

House Rules
A pair of words is given to each player. They must try to convert one word into the other in the fewest number of steps, changing only one letter at a time. For instance, to change 'dog' to 'cat', you might use the following steps:

DOG ➜ DOT ➜ COT ➜ CAT

This is pretty straightforward but the game gets more difficult as the words get longer, and by the time you get to six or seven letters it can get very tricky indeed!

Bulls and Cows

This is the predecessor of the better-known board game Mastermind, which was invented in 1971 by the wonderfully named Mordecai Meirowitz, a postmaster from Israel.

Stuff to Find
• Two players.
• Some paper and a pencil for each player.

House Rules
The players must decide who will be the code maker and the code breaker for the first game. The code maker must then choose four numbers from a group of eight (usually one to eight) and arrange them in a particular order. They must keep this code a secret.

The code breaker then has their first chance to crack the code and writes down their guess. After each guess the code maker provides feedback next to each number indicating the following:

- A coloured-in dot indicates that a number is both correct and in its correct position in the code.
- A circle indicates that the number does appear in the code but is not in the correct position.
- A cross indicates the number does not appear in the code.

Once feedback has been given, the code breaker guesses again, and keeps going until the code has been broken. The code maker wins a point for each incorrect guess. The winner is the player with the most points after a pre-agreed number of games has been played.

Variation
• • • • • • • •
- To make the game harder, you can allow duplicate numbers to be used, so a player could even choose the same four code numbers.
- To make the game faster (and more complicated!), the players could be both code maker and code breaker at the same time, trying to guess their opponent's code at the same time as providing feedback on the guesses for their own.

Who Am I?

Play time!

20 mins

This is another celebrity name-guessing game that is slightly easier for younger players as they can ask straightforward 'yes' or 'no' questions.

Stuff to Find
• At least four players.
• Some sticky notes or labels and some pens.

House Rules
All the players sit in a circle. Everyone writes down the name of a famous person on a piece of paper and sticks it to the forehead of the person next to them, without them seeing what it is. The idea is for all the players to be able to see everyone else's celebrity name apart from their own.

Each player then takes it in turns to ask the group 'yes' or 'no' questions to discover the name on their forehead. If the answer to their question is 'yes', they can ask another question but, if the answer is 'no', the turn passes to the player on their left. The first person to guess correctly is the winner.

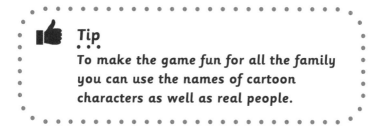
Variation

You can also stick the labels to people's backs and the game can be played in pairs. As before, the first player asks their partner a question, and, if the answer is 'yes' they get another go. If the answer is 'no', the second player gets to ask their questions. The first person to guess correctly is the winner.

Things Dads Say

'I am not running a taxi service!'

Jacks

Play time!
5–15 mins

This game is good, because it will keep everyone busy without creating too much mess.

Stuff to Find
• Ten metal jacks.
• A bouncy ball.

House Rules
The simplest way to play jacks is known as 'onesies'. Put all the jacks on your playing surface. Throw the ball up in the air and pick up one jack; keep the jack in your hand and catch the ball in the same hand when it has bounced once. Put this jack to one side and then repeat until all the jacks have been collected. If the ball bounces more than once before you pick up a jack, that is a foul.

After you have mastered onesies you can move on to twosies – picking up two jacks at a time – and so on, until you are picking up all ten jacks at once.

Variation
. . . .
To play in a group, the first player starts with onesies and keeps going until they foul. Play then moves to the next player. When the first player gets their next turn, they start where they left off the last time – if they missed on threesies, they start on threesies, etc. The first player to complete all levels is the winner.

Things Grandpas Say
. . . .
'The grass is always greener on the other side of the fence.'

Quiz Time
Sport

Sport often takes viewing precedence above everything else in our house – does that sound familiar?

1. Which well-known soccer player's surname is Luis Nazario de Lima?
2. Who was the first gymnast to be awarded a perfect 10 at the Olympic Games?
3. In which city does American football team the 49ers play?
4. Which cricketer holds the record for the greatest number of runs scored in a single innings in a test match?
5. In cycling, who has set a record by winning six Tours de France in succession?
6. What's the name of the game played on broomsticks by Harry Potter and his friends at Hogwarts?
7. What are the three disciplines in Three-day Eventing?
8. Which athletics discipline was revolutionised by Dick Fosbury?
9. What number shirt is worn by a fullback in Rugby Union?
10. In golf, what term is given to completing a hole in two shots under par?

Check the answers on pages 126–127.

Quiz Time
Answers

History p. 25
1. The Bayeux Tapestry
2. Rome
3. The Treaty of Versailles
4. Hippocrates
5. Charles I
6. Christopher Columbus
7. Delano
8. Three: Catherine of Aragon, Kathryn Parr and Katherine Howard
9. Russia
10. Korea

Science and Nature p. 45
1. Carbon
2. The femur (or thighbone)
3. Liquid Crystal Display
4. A Fibonacci Series
5. Protons and Neutrons
6. Lactose
7. The jaguar
8. X-rays
9. Cosine
10. Blue

Geography p. 65
1. The Balearic Islands
2. Peru
3. Washington DC
4. The Zambezi
5. The Dead Sea
6. An Oxbow lake
7. Singapore
8. Lebanon
9. The Indian Ocean
10. Gerard Mercator

Entertainment p. 85

1. 'Mad Men'
2. 'Goodfellas'
3. Bon Jovi
4. Montague and Capulet
5. Lt Theo Kojak
6. Russell Crowe
   ('Gladiator')
7. Aaron
8. Casablanca
9. Gustav Holst
10. Kasabian

Art and Literature p. 105

1. Jackson Pollock
2. 'Pride and Prejudice'
3. Auguste Rodin
4. King Lear
5. 'Little Women'
6. Frans Hals
7. The pilgrims in Chaucer's
   'The Canterbury Tales'
8. Aphrodite
9. Porcelain
10. Stephenie Meyer

Sport p. 125

1. Ronaldo
2. Nadia Comaneci (Montreal in
   1976)
3. San Francisco
4. Brian Lara (400 not out)
5. Lance Armstrong
6. Quidditch
7. Dressage, cross-country and
   show jumping
8. The high jump
9. 15
10. An Eagle

Acknowledgements

To me, games mean family, and I would like to thank mine for both testing out my carefully crafted instructions (I even found myself acting out the different signs for Charades to make sure I was describing them correctly), and for leaving me in peace while I attempted to get them down on paper. My five-year-old was delighted to be able to share the game Wink Murder with her friends at school. I am still waiting for my summons to the head teacher's office.

Thank you also to the friends and relations for all their encouragement and ideas. Finally, many thanks to Malcolm Croft, Rachel Malenoir and the team at Collins & Brown, for producing another lovely book.

Things Dads Say
. . . .
'Go and ask your mother.'